# VISUAL FUNK

## PSYCHEDELIC ADULT COLORING BOOK

ART BY JIM MAHFOOD

# ART BY JIM MAHFOOD

Editor and Book Design: Robbie Robbins
Publisher: Ted Adams

ISBN: 978-1-63140-545-7
WWW.IDWPUBLISHING.COM

Ted Adams, CEO Publisher
Greg Goldstein, President COO
Robbie Robbins, EVP/Sr. Graphic Artist
Chris Ryall, Chief Creative Officer/Editor-in-Chief
Matthew Ruzicka, CPA, Chief Financial Officer
Dirk Wood, VP of Marketing
Lorelei Bunjes, VP of Digital Services
Jeff Webber, VP of Licensing, Digital and Subsidiary Rights
Jerry Bennington, VP of New Product Development

For international rights, contact
licensing idwpublishing.com

19  18  17  16     2  3  4  5

Facebook: facebook.com/idwpublishing
Twitter: idwpublishing
YouTube: youtube.com/idwpublishing
Tumblr: tumblr.idwpublishing.com
Instagram: instagram.com/idwpublishing

This book belongs to

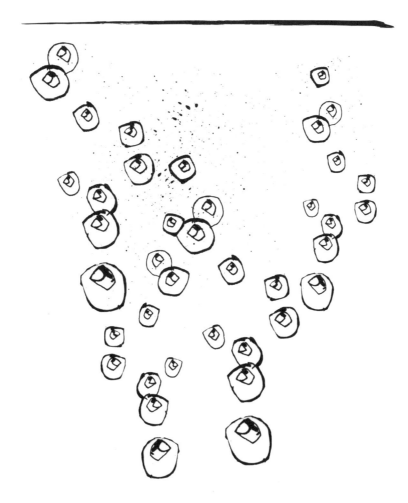

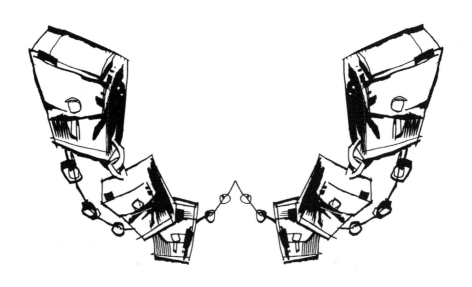

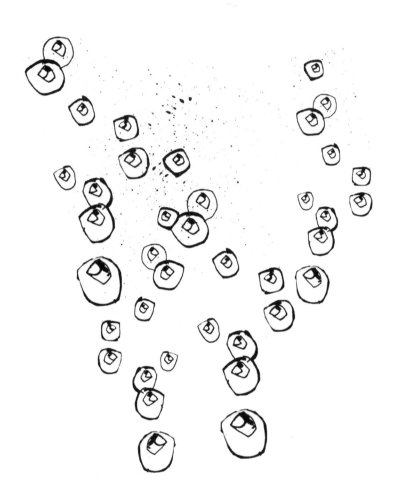

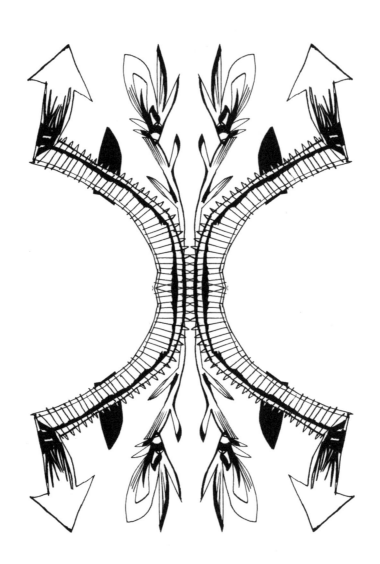

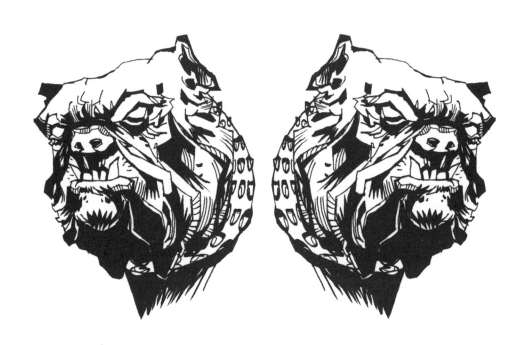

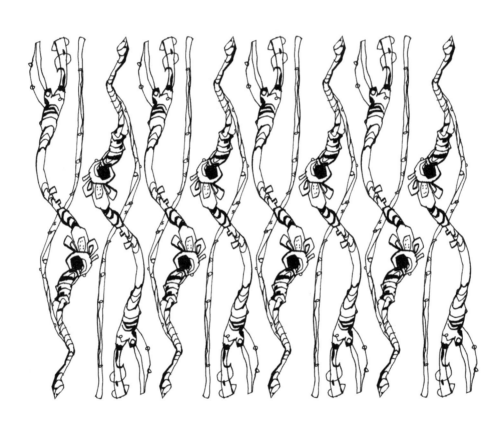

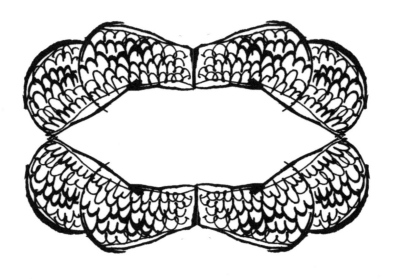

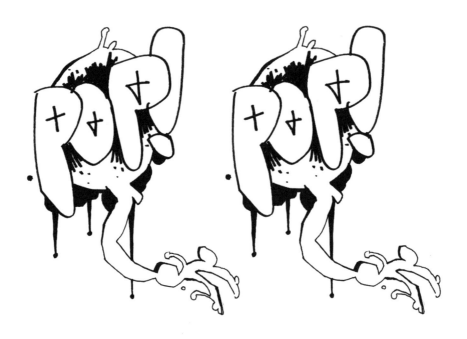

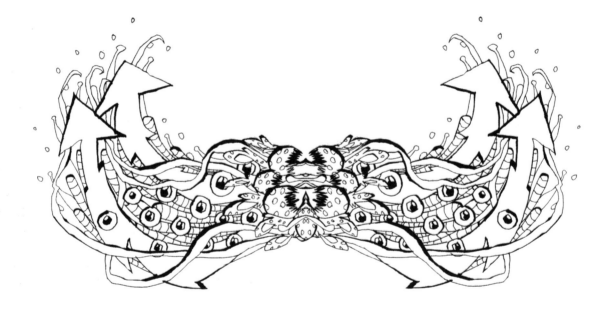

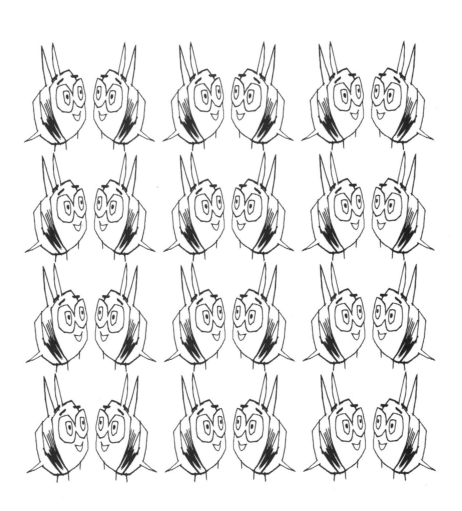

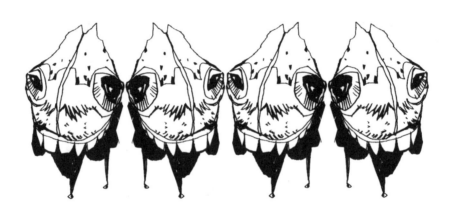

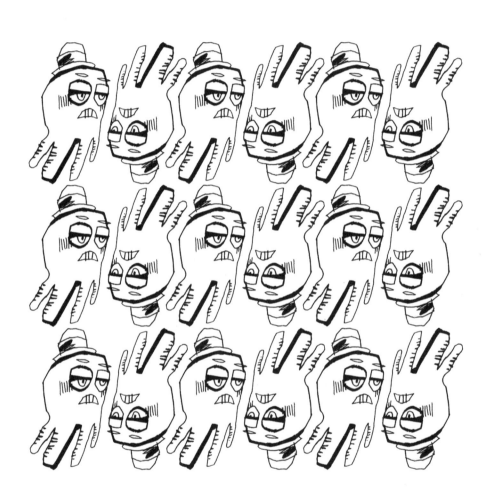

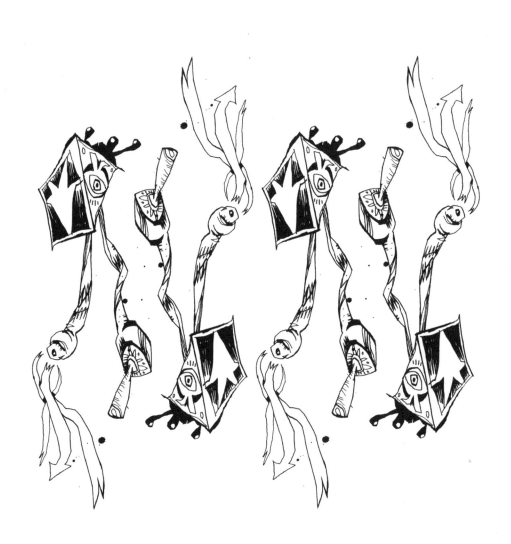

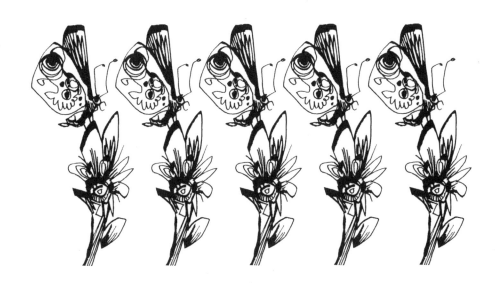

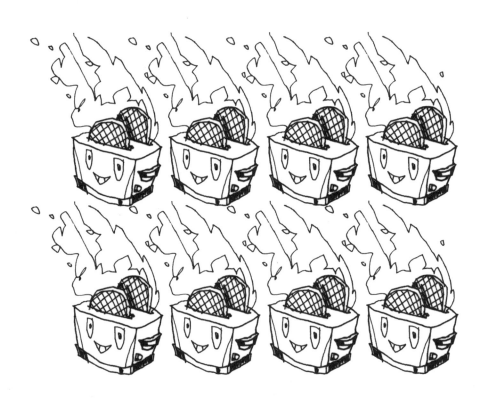